Children need love, security and a good relationship with at least one parent figure. Simple requirements you might think, but for a huge number of children these needs are not fulfilled. Far from it. During the past few years, society has slowly begun to recognise that relationships between children and adults can go disastrously wrong – sometimes violently wrong.

Child abuse is a difficult and harrowing subject. Although everyone agrees that child abuse exists, finding an exact definition is difficult. Generally, it involves a child or several children, an abuser or abusers, a family which can include the abuser, and it can be obvious or harder to uncover – as the following two examples shows. A young mother had a toddler who was teething. After several sleepless nights she lost her temper and threw the child across the room. The child hit his head on the corner of the table. Several hours later she took him to hospital where he was found to have a fractured skull. Another mother in a similar situation threw her child but he landed on the carpet. She ran out of the room leaving the child to cry and never told anyone about the incident. Both mothers abused their children, but only one admitted the fact.

This book looks at why children are abused and what can be done to stop this abuse. It looks at the victims, the abusers, the families and the procedures for dealing with abuse, or suspected abuse. It tries to understand some of the complex social and personal issues behind child abuse.

Most children are brought up in happy, loving families. But some are not. What goes wrong in a family where child abuse occurs and how can abuse be prevented?

UNDERSTANDING SOCIAL ISSUES

CHILD ABUSE

Angela Park

GLOUCESTER PRESS

London : New York : Toronto : Sydney

CHAPTER 1

WHAT IS CHILD ABUSE?

Child abuse is a
prison of fear and
lies. A child
abused is left with
scars that take a
long time to heal.
Some children
may never fully
recover unless
they receive help.

In Britain, 150-200 children die of child abuse or neglect every year. Thousands more suffer severe physical and emotional abuse and the number of reported cases of abuse is rising. However, no one knows for certain whether or not this is due to an increase in actual abuse, an increase in public awareness, or possibly both. The biggest increase has been in the number of reported cases of sexual abuse.

Everyone now agrees that there are several different types of child abuse, although the exact categories vary from country to country. In Britain five types of abuse are recognised. These are physical abuse, sexual abuse, neglect, emotional abuse and failure to thrive. Many children are vulnerable to more than one type of abuse. Mark, who is now six years old, was severely beaten by his father. It was an obvious case of physical abuse. Less obvious was the fact that he frequently went to school hungry and without having spoken to anyone since the day before.

Physical abuse
Physical abuse is the most widely recognised type of abuse. The range of injuries casued by physical violence is horrific – fatal and non fatal brain damage, broken bones, burns, bites and bruises are just some of the injuries suffered by children. Sometimes there may be tell tale signs like finger-mark bruises on the child's skin after the child has been severely shaken. But many injuries look like the result of everyday accidents or scrapes. Parents may use this fact to try and avoid suspicion or blame.

"His younger brother pushed him down the stairs."

To decide whether an injury is the result of physical abuse or not, many factors have to be considered. Is this the first time the child has suffered from this injury? Does the explanation offered by the parent fit the injury? Are the parents at all edgy? Was the child brought straight to hospital as soon as the injury was noticed, or was there a delay? Sometimes non-accidental injuries are caused by physical punishment. Many parents smack their children when they are naughty and, in general, a small amount of physical punishment is considered normal by Western societies.

Being abused makes a child feel different and very lonely. Sometimes it's difficult for an abused child to convince adults that what they say is true.

> "My dad and mum always gave me a good hiding when I was bad. It made me realise what was right and wrong".

But where do you draw the line between punishment and abuse? An American researcher found that most physical abuse in the United States was the result of a parent punishing a child physically in a manner which got out of control.

> "I only locked him in a trunk to teach him a lesson. He just won't listen to me."

Sexual abuse

Sexual abuse is now considered to be the most harmful type of abuse. There are three main areas of sexual abuse: incest – abuse within the family which could be abuse between children and their biological or step-parents; sexual abuse between a stranger and a child including paedophile abuse (a paedophile is someone who is strongly attracted to small children and who believes that sexual relations between adults and children are acceptable); and sexual exploitation – for example, the use of children in the making of pornographic films and books. Sometimes there isn't any evidence of sexual abuse. A child who has been photographed in the nude for a pornographic magazine shows no bruises. But suspicion may arise if a child has a sore bottom or bruising on the genitals. Or the behaviour of the child may give cause for concern. A child who is sexually precocious or excessively preoccupied with sexual matters may have been or is being abused. A very

withdrawn child, who lacks trust in men and feels worthless, may also be suffering sexual abuse.

Physical neglect
The neglected child who is under-fed, badly clothed and living in squalid conditions, is easy to identify. This is the image of child abuse that many children's charities use to publicise their work. But physical neglect can range from this obvious picture to one which is harder to identify. Many children are physically neglected just by being left alone.

All children need reassurance especially younger ones. Being left alone can be a frightening experience even if someone is in the next room. Being cold, hungry and afraid of being hurt is terrifying.

"I only popped out for a quick drink. How did I know he would climb out of his cot and play with the electric socket."

Alongside physical neglect there is emotional neglect. The toddler who is regularly abandoned at night will feel frightened and uncared for. Emotional neglect is difficult to assess. It may include failure to provide stimulation, or love, or maybe just failure to provide a routine to a child's life.

> "My mum allows me to go out anytime. She doesn't care. She's always in bed watching television. I get my own food – steal it sometimes."

Children take up a great deal of time. They need to be talked to, played with, cared for and given attention. Without this attention, children fail to thrive.

Failure to thrive

Some children grow more slowly as a consequence of neglect. This is called growth retardation, or more often, "failure to thrive". Failure to thrive sometimes indicates that another type of abuse is also taking place. For example, in "Munchausen

by proxy syndrome", the abused child is smaller than other children of the same age. In this syndrome a mother frequently causes, or imagines, her child to be ill. She may use drugs and poisons to produce symptoms of illness in the child.

Emotional abuse

Emotional abuse is the most difficult category of abuse to define. It can lead to failure to thrive and it is certainly part of sexual abuse, neglect and physical abuse. It is so closely linked to these other types of abuse that some countries don't acknowledge it as a separate form of abuse. The term covers a range of abuse from unrealistic demands for academic achievement to mental degradation.

> **"My mum makes me work for four hours after school every day. At weekends I only get a couple of hours play. She says I'll thank her when I get older. But whatever I do, she's never satisfied."**

Age and sex differences

The average age of physically and emotionally abused children is approximately six years. The average age of a sexually abused child is approximately ten years and four-fifths of those children registered as being abused in Britain in 1986 were girls. The neglected child's average age is four years and the failure to thrive only one year. But the usefulness of these figures is limited. There are one year olds being sexually abused and 15 year olds being physically abused.

CHAPTER 2

NOTICING ABUSE

In some parts of
the world children
may accept it as
normal that they
should work for a
living. But
working long
hours and in
unpleasant
conditions stunts
their growth both
physically and
mentally.

The problem of child abuse has not suddenly appeared over the last century. Accounts of children being abused go back as far as history. Children's fairy tales and folk tales include many stories of children being abused. Most of these stories have a happy ending - Cinderella and Hansel and Gretel finally escape their abusers. Yet most of these stories are inaccurate as the abusers often appear as a wicked stepmother or witch. Today we know from research findings that men are far more likely to be the abusers of children than women.

Recent history
In the 1980s we accept that children have a right to childhood and a right to be protected from experiences which could damage them both physically and emotionally. However, in the last century the position of children was very different. Children were expected to work long hours, made to climb up smoke-filled chimneys, made to crawl down mines, mend dangerous machines, beaten, starved, and even sold as slaves. All children were considered to be the property of their parents and in poor families it was often necessary for even very young children to earn their keep.

Mary Ellen's Story
How did Britain and the United States come to recognise the problem of child abuse? The story began in 1875 with a little girl called Mary Ellen who lived in New York in a district known as Hell's Kitchen. The woman who lived next door to Mary Ellen could hear her being beaten. The

neighbour fell seriously ill and was visited by a missionary worker. She implored the missionary worker to help the girl next door. The missionary worker went to the police for help but they refused to intervene. So did the magistrates, various charitable organisations and prominent citizens. Finally she turned to Henry Bergh the founder of the New York Society for the Prevention of Cruelty to Animals. They tried to find a law that would allow them to remove the child from her home but there was not one.

Eventually they decided to act as if the child was an animal. Officers from the animal protection society went to the house and removed the child along with the scissors which had been used to slash her whole body. They brought her before the Supreme Court wrapped in a horse blanket. When

These children worked in a cotton mill in the United States at the turn of the century. In some parts of the world, many children still work – often in bad conditions.

the newspapers reported the incident the general public was shocked. As a result of the case the Society for the Protection of Cruelty to Children was set up in New York. A similar society was opened in Britain in 1883.

Medical evidence for abuse

For some time pathologists (doctors who try to establish the cause of death by examining bodies) had noticed old fractures in the bodies of abused children examined in postmortems. These fractures hadn't been noted by family doctors. Then, in the 1920s when X-rays began to be used to help establish the cause of death, scientists noticed that these old fractures could be distinguished from those caused accidently. Brain swelling – a result of severe shaking which can lead to death or brain damage – was also observed.

The Battered Baby Syndrome

In 1962 the paediatrician Henry Kempe and fellow workers described the "Battered Baby Syndrome". As a result of his work, doctors have become more skilled in recognising the physical signs of abuse. Today the term battered baby has become a household word describing a phenomenon which eveyone recognises. Kempe also outlined six stages of awareness that communities go through in their understanding of the issues of child abuse. These stages are useful for assessing other countries' the many workers involved in different types of child abuse cases.

THE SIX STAGES OF RECOGNISING CHILD ABUSE

1 *Denial that abuse is significant or widespread and a belief that it is only carried out by drug-crazed parents.*
2 *The community begins to take note of the more brutal forms of abuse such as battering.*
3 *The recognition of more subtle forms of abuse such as neglect and failure to thrive.*
4 *The recognition of emotional neglect and abuse, and concern about effects of rejection and scapegoating of children by parents.*
5 *The slow and painful recognition of the existence of sexual abuse.*
6 *The belief that every child has the right to be wanted and to receive proper food, health care and loving attention.*

Child abuse throughout the world

Countries vary in their ability and willingness to recognise child abuse. Different cultures and child-rearing patterns also complicate the picture. For example, Japan insists that physical abuse is not a problem. Japanese children are thought to cry less and be more passive. But problems emerge as these children get older. The many teenage suicides in Japan are thought to be a result of tremendous pressures put on children to succeed academically.

In Sweden it is against the law to smack or punish your child physically. In the United States, Britain and many other countries the use of physical punishment to control a child is considered normal. In the Netherlands parents are described as "mishandling" their children, rather than abusing them. Underlying this shift in emphasis is the idea that some parents need help in order to learn to handle their children better. As they can't learn to do this if the family is split up or the abuser is imprisoned, the abuser is punished with imprisonment only as a last resort. The Netherlands considers sexual neglect – a parent's refusal to educate their children in sexual matters – to be a form of mishandling. Teaching children to be ashamed of their bodies is another form of mishandling.

Should other countries include these types of mishandling in their definition of child abuse? A lot depends on the material conditions in the country. Many countries believe they have more

pressing problems of health and nutrition and so educational or sexual neglect would fall low on their list of priorities. Others believe that the Dutch views on mishandling interfere with the family's right to bring up children free from the worry that the state might intervene.

The worst conditions

In many parts of the world the child mortality rate is high. Children are dying from disease and malnutrition as a result of drought, famine and war. Efforts are concentrated on feeding these children to keep them alive. Nevertheless some governments are working towards ways of dealing with the abuse these children often suffer on top of their desperate material plight. Relief agencies such as Oxfam are also helping.

By the 1960s the battered baby syndrome was widely recognised. A crying baby is stressful for every parent but if help is at hand then abuse is less likely.

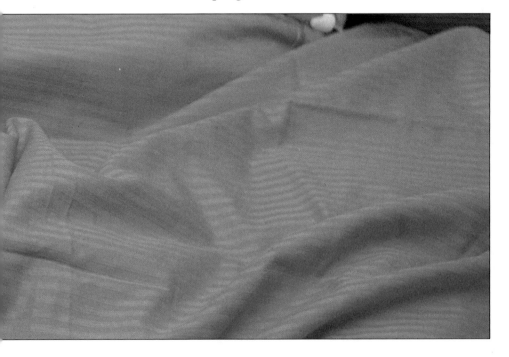

CASE STUDY

Philip is an 11 year old boy. He is on the skinny side but tall like his father. He comes from a good family, his father has his own printing business. Three years ago the family split up. Philip stayed in the family home with his mother and his younger sister Susan. Philip has always done well at school.

After the split up Philip's mother had many boyfriends. But after about a year she met John. John was everything that Philip's father was not. He didn't have a steady job. He took the family on wild outings and did crazy outrageous things. At first Philip liked John. He brought him presents and he enjoyed the outings. He hadn't seen his mother laugh so much for years. Then John moved in to live with Philip and his mother and sister. At first things went well. Then John lost his job and began to stay in the house more and he began to drink.

Philip's mother had worked part time after the family split up but after John lost his job she took a full time job in order to support John as well. This meant that John was supposed to look after Philip and his sister when they came home from school. As time went on John became more and more gloomy. Philip took over looking after Susan when they got home while John watched television.

Then John began to pick on Philip. First he was too noisy then he was too quiet, always creeping about. Then Philip left his books on the floor, then on the table. Philip's friends stopped coming to the house because he was never allowed out by John. When he complained to his mother she just said it was for his own good. Finally one day John flew at Susan for not eating her food. Philip had had enough. He shouted at John not to speak to Susan that way because he was not her dad. John grabbed hold of Philip and smashed him against the wall. He nearly beat him unconscious.

When Philip's mother came home John immediately told her

that Philip had been fighting. After the incident nothing much happened between Philip and John. Philip began to feel that John was scared that his mother would find out and so it wouldn't happen again. But it did. This time John twisted Philip's arm, held a knife to his throat and stuffed his head down the toilet.

Several times Philip phoned his father who was always too busy to talk to him. It wasn't until Philip's sister accidentally told a friend about life at home and a teacher overheard that anything was done to help Philip. John has left the home and both Philip's father and mother are now trying to help their son overcome his experience.

CHAPTER 3

THE VICTIMS

Abused children come from all types of homes. Some children who are brought up in poor conditions live happy and safe family lives. Other children may live in fine houses but are abused.

All children are exposed to the risk of child abuse at sometime in their lives. The park, the street, the playground can all be dangerous places for a child. But are some children more likely to be abused than others? A lot of research has been carried out in an attempt to identify those situations and background factors which place a family, or a child, at a greater risk. However it is important to realise that even in families where risk factors are present, it does not automatically mean that the children are, or will be, abused. Many children are brought up in extreme conditions but are not exposed to abuse. Others who come from "good" homes, at least on the surface, are chronically abused.

Background risk factors

Children are more at risk from physical abuse in families where there is unemployment or the main wage earner is a manual worker and where there is a conflict between the parents. This is also true for children in the failure to thrive group. Neglect is often a problem in a single parent family. Sexual abuse occurs in families from all backgrounds but children are particularly at risk from stepfathers and if one of the adults in the family were themselves sexually abused as children. Stepfathers and boyfriends are implicated in 19 per cent of injury cases and 25 per cent of sex abuse cases. Natural fathers are implicated in a third of sex abuse cases, compared with three per cent of mothers.

A baby's birth weight can also be a very important background risk factor. Low birth

Premature children are at greater risk of abuse because their parents find it difficult to feel close to such a small baby. They often feel unable to cuddle them and see them as backward compared to other children.

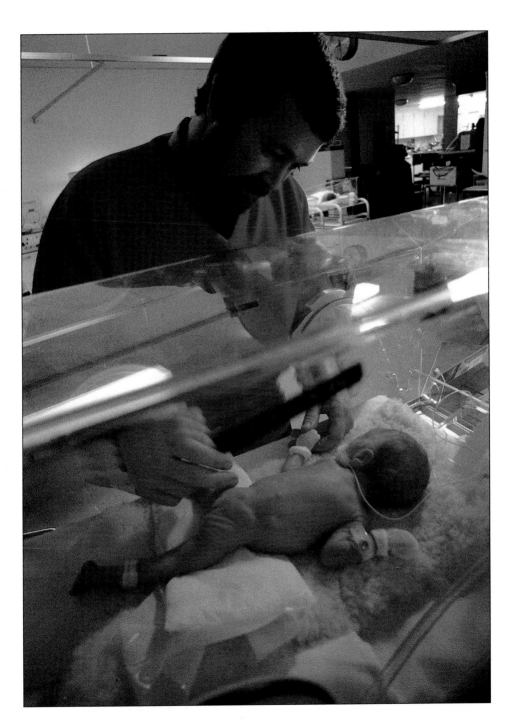

weight or premature babies are more likely to be born into a family suffering poverty, or to young teenage mothers. Premature babies are often separated from their mothers immediately after birth because they need intensive care and this may result in the baby being less responsive and having feeding difficulties. It may be unwell and need further time in hospital. This can start a vicious circle whereby the child's illness results in it being considered backward for its age. Low birth weight children are more likely to suffer physical abuse, neglect and failure to thrive, but not sexual abuse.

Another group for whom abuse is often a reality is the mentally handicapped. They, even more than other groups, cannot defend themselves against abuse. Runaways and children who are abducted are also high risk groups. They are particularly vulnerable to sexual abuse and exploitation. Ironically, the majority of runaways are fleeing from homes where they have been abused. Often those who were sexually abused at home end up as prostitutes. Now, along with the other problems they face, they risk contracting AIDS which may add, in an indirect way, to the number of children who die from abuse.

Death from abuse

No one knows exactly how many children die from abuse. There may be a suspicion that the child was killed but perhaps not enough evidence to convict the murderer. Nor do deaths from abuse statistics include those children who die from illnesses from which they could have recovered had they not

been weakened by abuse. Reports in the newspapers about child deaths are met with shock and recrimination yet there are many more children whose deaths go unnoticed by the national press. For some of these children death may have been a thankful release.

Recording children's fingerprints helps trace missing children in the United States. Thousands of children go missing every year.

> **"It shouldn't hurt to be a child but sometimes it does."**

Reacting to abuse . . .

Physically abused children vary in the way they respond to abuse. Some children will try hard to avoid further abuse while others seem to invite the abuse they dread. The avoidant child will be anxious, sensitive and may be over compliant. All behaviour is directed to what is uppermost in the child's mind – a desperate attempt to avoid further blows. In this type of behaviour, sometimes called "frozen watchfulness", the child is over attentive like a cat watching its prey – only this time the child is the prey.

> **"She did everything her mother asked and stood by the door all the time we had tea. She never seemed to take her eyes off her mother. It was really strange 'cos she's only two years old."**

The inviting child on the other hand will be very active, clumsy, careless and will often have accidents. In long-term abuse, a child may stop enjoying things usually enjoyed by children. They may show "pseudo-mature behaviour" and act like a grown up. This type of behaviour is most often associated with neglect and emotional abuse. A child who is looking after two younger children while her mother is high on drugs will forget to play. Instead her time is taken up feeding, washing and caring for her younger brothers and sisters. Some children react to physical abuse with symptoms that may be noticed by the child's teacher or doctor. Tantrums, hyperactivity, bed-wetting, problems at school, withdrawn behaviour, aggression, self-destructive and compulsive behaviour such as constant eating, can all be signs that a child is being abused at home.

The neglected child may well show some of the same signs of distress as the physically abused child. But in the case of the neglected child, the most obvious sign of distress is the lack of physical development. The emotionally abused child may have any of the above problems, or a combination of them.

Reacting to sexual abuse

Children who have been sexually abused often show distressed behaviour which is like that of victims of other types of abuse. But children who have been sexually abused often blame themselves for what is happening. Furthermore, victims are often blamed by their families or abusers for the fact that abuse has taken place.

> **"Children are very sexy, they ask for it."**

But how can children be blamed or blame themselves for the sexual perversion and abuse of trust by an adult? The adult is always responsible, no matter how the child responds to the abuse. Most abusers know this but many will go to great

All children are vulnerable, whatever their background or circumstances. It is impossible to predict which child will be abused and which one will not. However girls are more vulnerable to sexual abuse than boys.

lengths to avoid admitting it. Blaming a child is an easy way out but if the child accepts the blame it leads to a tremendous burden of guilt for that child. Abused victims of all types of abuse often have crippling feelings of worthlessness and low self-esteem.

"If only I hadn't gone to the park alone that afternoon. I knew that man was weird when he asked me to play games in the morning."

Keeping the family secret . . .

Sexual abuse victims end up with battered feelings as a result of abuse. These feelings arise because of the confusion created by the abuse. Secrecy plays a large part. If the abuser says "we mustn't tell Mummy or she will be cross", the child comes to fear that she has done something wrong and will be punished – even if she doesn't know why. Feeling helpless is part of an abused child's reality. Joan, a 12 year old, who had been abused by her stepfather over many months felt it was impossible to stand up to him; it is difficult for a child to protect herself against continuing abuse and to stand up to a parent's authority. Most children don't cry for help unless they have been taught self-protection. In some families, the child is made responsible for keeping the family together and abusers will go to enormous lengths to frighten a child into silence.

"Daddy told me that if I told anyone enormous snakes which he had put there would come out of my belly and eat me up."

Believing the child

Research has shown that children are no more prone to lying than adults. So why do many people confronted with a disclosure of sexual abuse reject it? In general, workers and the public can accept that children are being battered. Most parents can identify with feelings of violent exasperation towards their kids – even if they haven't battered them. But very few will admit to sexual feelings towards their children and therefore find it hard to believe others have these feelings and actually act them out.

CHAPTER 4

THE ABUSER

Abusers are
fathers, mothers,
friends and
relations. Only
occasionally are
they strangers.
Ninety per cent of
sexual abuse is
committed by
men – men and
women physically
abuse and neglect
children equally.

Who are the abusers of children? The popular idea of the abuser or abusive family is of a "sick" individual or family, living in squalid circumstances where violence, alcohol and drugs are part of everyday life. This is true in some instances but it is far from typical. Although some risk factors may make someone more likely to abuse a child, there simply isn't a stereotypical abuser. Similarities between abusers can be divided into two categories, those connected with personality and those connected with background. The background factors, such as unemployment, are similar and have been discussed in the previous chapter.

The physically abusive individual is often isolated, lacking in knowledge of parenting, self-righteous and impulsive. These are all characteristics of outward behaviour. Inwardly he is confused, frustrated, often powerless outside the family and dependent. The conflict between how he is in the outside world and what he feels can lead him to become unpredictable and unstable.

> **"Being a battered child means hoping your parents will be in a good mood, but knowing you couldn't trust them even if they were."**

Inwardly, the neglectful parent is similar to the physically abusive parent – he is untrusting, feels persecuted, often depressed and worried about himself. Outwardly these parents appear self-sufficient. The emotionally abusing individual also appears self-sufficient and remains detached and critical of the world. He is unable to cope with his feelings of frustration and stress and is hopelessly inadequate at dealing with his children's emotional needs. These people often feel that they are victims of society and are often very suspicious of offers of help.

The sexual abuser is different. He is often moralistic and uses intellectual and rational arguments to explain his behaviour. This is particularly true of those sexual abusers from outside the family such as paedophiles and strangers who trick children into abusive situations.

> **"Kids are just like adults. They want sex the way we do. Just because they can't get married doesn't stop them wanting sex."**

Sexual abusers are often inadequate sexually, shy, and have feelings of powerlessness outside the family – and sometimes within the family too. Talking about matters is rare and secrets abound. Often mothers are accused of turning a blind eye to sexual abuse. The mother may sometimes be glad and relieved that her daughter is meeting her husband's needs. Should they be blamed for "allowing" the situation to develop in the first place? Those who have turned a "blind eye" may also be subjected to both physical and sexual abuse by the abuser.

Outside the family

The sex offender from outside the family has a different profile although there are some similarities with an abusive parent. These people, again usually men, are addicted to abuse. It is estimated that a paedophile will have abused approximately 70 children before he is caught. But in some cases the number of children abused by one person may

Children can use drawings to help them to tell adults about what has happened to them. Sometimes their story may be too painful to put into words – or they may be too young to even know how to describe what has happened to them.

run into the thousands. A paedophile may spend his life trying to get access to children and may work in a job which brings him into contact with children.

Some individuals who abuse children physically or who neglect their children have a low intelligence. But this is not the case in sexual child abuse. The person who abuses a child sexually is just as likely to be of high intelligence as of low intelligence, to come from a rich background as a poor background. In a 1988 report published in Britain, it was found that natural fathers were involved in a third of sexual abuse cases, stepfathers and boyfriends who lived with the child's biological mother were involved in a quarter of the cases, while almost one in three of the children were sexually abused by brothers, mothers' boyfriends or neighbours.

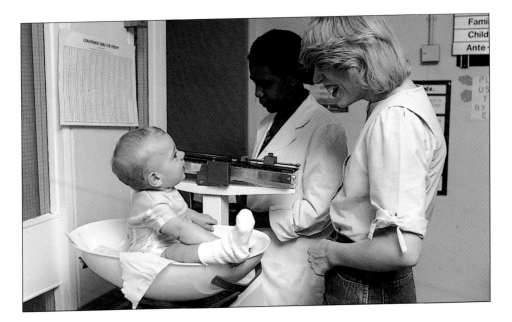

Cycle of abuse

One background factor alone is of little value in predicting who will be an abuser. Yet some evidence indicates that an abused child will grow up to abuse his children in a "cycle of abuse". However this is not the case in sexual abuse – the majority of sexually abused victims are girls and the majority of abusers are men. However, some evidence suggests that a woman who has been sexually abused as a child may be attracted to an abusive type of man and this may lead to the sexual abuse of her own daughters and sons.

Regular check-ups and visits to the doctor are important ways of monitoring a young child's health and growth. A baby's weight and height indicate if the child is thriving.

Coping without much help

Another group at high risk of being abusive is single parents, especially those who are socially isolated. They lack someone to turn to when the stresses and strains become unmanageable. Teenage parents, especially those who have their first child during adolescence, are at the highest risk of being abusive – usually physically abusing their children. Those at greatest risk of neglecting their children have large families with children of a young age and not much money at a time when their friends have few family commitments and more money to spend on themselves. Failure to thrive children may also have young, isolated parents.

Trying to find an explanation

Why do parents or individuals abuse children? Abuse is much easier to understand if it can be pinned down to some thing – such as depression after a baby has been born, bad parenting or a family in which all the roles are chaotic.

> **"I tried to settle her. I did everything I could think of but she still kept on crying. I just shook her and shook her. I wanted her to be quiet."**

Most types of abuse seem to involve the abuser's need for power and control over others. The abuser who often feels helpless outside the family can exert his authority over the family's weaker members, sometimes releasing his frustrations and anger on them. Alternatively he uses them self-consciously for his own needs and controls them with threats and fear. In a family where one child becomes the scapegoat – the target for abuse – the other parent may eventually also release their frustrations with the situation on that same child.

Who is the child murderer?

It would be foolish to say that there is a typical child murderer. There simply isn't. But we can look at the profile of those who have been convicted of murder. The majority are male, not the natural father, recently imprisoned or with a criminal record involving violence, unemployed and caring for the child while the mother works. Drug and alcohol abuse may be a feature. In some cases the mother is also convicted of murder or found to be party to the crime. She is most likely to be either pregnant or has just given birth, has several children under four and to be of low intelligence and poorly educated.

> **"I wanted him to appreciate what I was doing for him," said a father who murdered his two year old son. He had four jobs to support his family and spent some of his day looking after the children.**

Society's response to the abuser is, on the whole, punitive. Most people consider child abuse to be the worst crime of all. Child molesters and child murderers are separated from other prisoners because of threats on their life. But should we punish these people and if so how? Whatever the answer, it is necessary to understand them because this is the only way to prevent abuse from continuing.

CASE STUDY

Sarah is a pretty seven year old child. She has blonde hair, blue eyes and is quite small for her age. Her mother, Helen, gave birth to Sarah when she was only 18. Sarah's father, Mike is much older. He left school as soon as he could and since then has worked in labouring jobs – when he can find one. He has never earned much money.

The family used to have their own flat. But Sarah's mother, Helen, finds it difficult to manage money properly so, when Sarah was four, they left the flat because of debts and moved in with Helen's parents, Bill and Joyce. Bill often helped put Sarah to bed while Helen helped Joyce with the evening meal. One evening Bill was bathing Sarah when she began crying. Neither Sarah's mother or father could calm her. Finally she cried herself to sleep. The following day when Sarah's mother was making Sarah's bed she found blood on her nightdress. That night Sarah would not let Bill bath her.

Sarah's mother decided that they had to leave. She told her parents that they had the chance of getting a flat if they left the area. In fact, they moved in with the other grandparents who lived in another area. Norman and Dora, Mike's parents, where surprised by the move but wanted to help the family find their own place. Sarah settled down a bit more and began to go to the local school.

After six months Sarah started to get stomach aches. Her mother took her to the doctor on several occasions. The doctor could find nothing wrong. Sarah also refused to go to school. She became very clinging and wouldn't leave her mother's side. She began to irritate her mother. Dora suggested that Sarah may be being bullied at school. So, Sarah's mother went to see her teacher after school. The teacher was concerned about Sarah but mainly because she was so quiet in the class. The teacher said she would keep an eye open in case she was being bullied in the playground.

Things did not improve. Sarah began to refuse food and became difficult in class. One night she woke screaming. Sarah's mother found it difficult to calm her. Finally she cried, "Please stop grandpa touching me". Sarah then told of how Norman came into her room at night and lay on top of her. Dora was stunned. Sarah's mother began to cry. When Dora confronted Norman, he broke down and retreated to his room. The rest of the family tried to decide what to do. They didn't want to phone the police so phoned the local social services department. A social worker came immediately. She suggested that either Norman should leave or Sarah should be removed from the home whilst an investigation was carried out. Sarah's mother and father agreed that Sarah should go.

CHAPTER 5

THE PROCESS OF HELPING

Some parents may have to manage in difficult circumstances, working hard to bring up children with love and affection despite bad housing and poverty. But bad conditions can increase the risk of some types of abuse.

What happens when someone thinks a child is being abused, or a child or parent asks for help? The help available varies from country to country. Often there isn't enough evidence to prove that abuse has taken place and no conclusion can be reached. In situations like this, the risks facing the children have to be assessed. Initially this is done by a social worker, or some other professional worker assigned to the family for welfare reasons.

Getting it right . . .

If the risk is assessed incorrectly and a child is seriously abused again, or even killed as sometimes happens, the workers can be held legally responsible. If, on the other hand, the worker is sure that abuse has occurred and it hasn't, then separation of the family will cause severe unnecessary stress and hardship. Even the label "abused child" can be damaging. In cases where no bruises are to be seen how is the decision reached? Fortunately workers are increasingly aware of the fact that what children tell them is true.

> **"I knew the parents were lying and just saying it for my benefit. They thought I was a stupid interfering social worker who wanted to split up their family for the hell of it."**

But piecing the child's story together may be a slow and painful process; some children are unable to talk about their experiences or need much encouragement to do so. It may take some children many weeks before they begin to tell their story.

Family privacy

What rights do the family have in situations where children are considered to be at risk from abuse? If suspicions are only based on another person's word and not proven, they may be very hurtful and disturbing. A parent will feel helpless and confused by alleged sexual abuse especially if the initial story comes from someone with a grudge against the family. So it may be necessary to protect the parent. But more important is the complicated task of working out how much to believe of the parent's story. First of all, the worker needs to collect as many facts about the family as possible. Secondly, they need to get to know every member of the family as closely as possible. There may be a series of interviews held between the social worker and the parents.

The abused child lives a life of loneliness. It may seem impossible for her to tell her story to an adult – especially if she is worried that talking about abuse will split up the family.

The professional helpers . . .
There are many professionals involved in cases of child abuse – doctors, health visitors, psychiatrists, psychologists and psycho-therapists, lawyers and judges, social workers, teachers and the police. In some countries special agencies have been set up to deal with child abuse, for example the NSPCC (National Society for the Prevention of Cruelty to Children) in Great Britain.

"Our aim is to remove the evil from the home, not the child."

A cry for help
The process of helping begins with a cry for help, or an expression of concern from someone outside the family. Most cases of abuse are, in fact, reported by the general public. If abuse is obvious then protecting the child is easy to effect. When a worker visits a family and finds a child in distress they can arrange for a "place of safety order" to be issued by a magistrate. This order allows the child to be removed from the family immediately but for a limited amount of time. If the abuse is not obvious then an investigation begins which is carried out by a social worker. The police will carry out a separate investigation if a prosecution is to be made. In cases of sexual abuse both the police and the social worker will work together.

Who should leave the family home to stop or prevent the abuse? Workers are trying to keep families together or, if necessary, remove the abuser – not the child.

Splitting up the family
When should children be separated from their parents? A place of safety order is only for a short period so once it has expired, the decision has to be

made about whether the child should return to its parents. Sometimes a care order is granted by the court. This has longer-term powers than a place of safety order and the local authority rather than the parents then become legally responsible for the care of the child. The child is taken into care for shorter or longer periods of time; a full care order lasts until the child is 18 years old. A care order is usually granted by a judge if the child is being abused, exposed to moral danger, or being neglected in anyway. A care order may also be issued if a member of the household has been convicted of abuse of a child. Sometimes the worker may not have enough evidence to obtain a care order. For example, a retarded child may not be able to relate his story and there is no physical evidence of abuse. In this situation, the worker may apply to

Workers have to weigh up the advantages and disadvantages of keeping the family together or placing the child in care. Family centres, like the one in the photograph, may provide a welcome alternative.

the high court to make the child a "ward" of court.

When a child is under a care order all parental rights are removed. The social worker can place the child where they think best. This might be at home or in foster care, in a children's home, or with another member of the extended family. They can also decide how often the parent can see the child. Once a child has been placed in care, they can only be removed from the children's home or returned to the family home, with the permission of the court.

"There are some abusers who will never change and removing them from society is the only way of dealing with them."

Keeping the family together

There is an important debate going on among all those who work in the area of child abuse. Should their aim be to keep the family together if at all possible, or should they break up the family in order to give the child a fresh start? Most workers would agree that keeping the family together is the better alternative even though in a few cases this has proved fatal. Breaking up the family is what the sexually abused child fears most. Many of these children keep the family secret because they are afraid that if they told someone about the abuse, it would mean the end of their family life. The effects of long term fostering and adoption must be balanced against the risk of further abuse. Family centres and compulsory child-minding can provide a useful alternative to the break up of the family. At the centre children are regularly monitored and parents encouraged to come to play with their children. This gives them the opportunity to learn parenting skills, discuss their problems and help in the everyday running of the centre.

All sorts of therapy are thought to be of value for abusive families. Unfortunately though long term effects are only achieved with long term therapy. Therapy can be useful in helping the mother and father to have a better relationship. It can also help the abused child to come to terms with their experience and express any anger or feelings towards the parents – "I never told anyone that my father abused me. They wouldn't have believed me anyway. Now that I have had therapy, I realise that it was his fault. I always blamed myself. I have even told my husband and it has brought us much closer. He understands my feelings and moods much better now. I'm not cured. That will never happen but I can cope most of the time."

Finally a word must be said about the people who work in the area of abuse.

"It knocked me back for weeks. I kept asking myself could I have handled this dreadful case differently."

Many workers leave because of "emotional burn out". They become hardened to the heartbreak of abuse and are in danger of missing clues. This hardening is often the result of over-involvement in the situation. Training and specialist advice can help to cut down the anxiety of working with very distressed children but sometimes the feelings of anger, frustration and despair may overwhelm the worker so that they feel they cannot continue to

> **"Some abusers show total remorse and more damage could be done by splitting up the family."**

work in the area. Perhaps the best way to understand the workers' feelings is to read the case histories included in this book. How would you feel talking to an abuser? How would you react if a child told you the details of severe neglect or sexual abuse?

Many children need a great deal of patience and support before they can trust an adult with their story. Sometimes the child will only tell their story once – and then try to forget the painful details.

CHAPTER 6

THE FUTURE – CAN ABUSE BE PREVENTED?

Abuse can be prevented by taking positive action. Every mother-to-be needs support to make her baby welcome and to make sure that she has the resources to cope with the stresses and strains of being a mother.

For children and adults who have come into contact with child abuse, the consequences are very real. For others who hear about it through newspapers, books or on television, it is something that only happens to other people. But in fact, every child is a potential victim and every adult a potential abuser.

It is not hard to begin to imagine what it is like to be abused. Everyone experiences moments of rejection during their childhood – moments of frustration, powerlessness and fear. But what if childhood felt like that all the time? What if those feelings are only the tip of the iceberg? How would you feel if a loved adult interfered with you in a way that you didn't like?

> **"I just wanted someone to cuddle me without hurting me."**

Understanding child abuse will help prevent it. Turning a blind eye won't. The community as a whole can help prevent child abuse further by caring. Comments such as "It's none of my business" or "they need a good thrashing" are heard only too often. Even those who dislike children or who have nothing to do with them were once vulnerable children themselves.

Caring for others

Caring can mean many different things. It may just mean supporting a local playgroup, making sure children have safe places to play or volunteering to have a handicapped child for a day in order to take the pressure off the parents. Communities must be aware of their isolated members such as single parents. Babysitting services can allow a single parent a break and a chance to make other friends or develop new interests. It is easy to condemn those who abuse children. It is much harder to recognise ways of helping.

> **"Lots of my school friends came round when I first had the baby. I don't see them much now. I know they have exams. I just wish occasionally one would babysit so I could go out. I wouldn't feel so trapped if I could go out once in a while."**

Helplines

In some countries more formal help and support is available. There are telephone helplines for children, parents and adults who were abused as children and members of the public who are concerned. In 1986 ChildLine opened in Britain amidst much publicity. In the first 48 hours it received approximately 5,000 calls. The organisers were staggered by the response and amazed at the numbers of children needing to tell someone about what was happening to them. Any adult can help a child in distress just by believing what they are telling them about being abused. Listening and then helping the child to get professional help will help the child come to terms with their experience.

> **"When she first told me I wanted to run away and cry. But she wasn't crying. Then I realised how much courage she had in telling me and I knew I had to help her."**

Schools help children by teaching them how to protect themselves. Children are taught to

Children born to mothers who have been abused may feel that their mothers cannot touch and cuddle them as they would like. In this painting a child has shown the mother as separate to the rest of the family.

differentiate between "good" and "bad" touches and to talk to trusted adults. Once children feel there is support for their problem and feel they can talk, then the abuser can be identified and helped.

Long-term help

Society is making efforts to deal with the problem of abuse. Countries that are better off are helping those less well off. The courts are recognising the needs of children and the difficulties of bringing abusers to justice. New ways of presenting a child's evidence to the court are being researched and video links may be used more widely so that the child does not have to appear in court. Doctors and therapists are researching better ways of helping families and victims overcome their experiences. Social workers are trying not to separate

families – instead they aim to support them and change their behaviour.

Perhaps the most important thing to remember is that there is no perfect way to bring up a child and each child is different. Each abuser is different too, and the way to help an abused family varies greatly depending on the type of abuse and the reactions of the abuser.

At last governments are putting more resources into working to prevent child abuse and to help its victims. And, at long last, it is now fully recognised that child abuse can scar a human being for the rest of their life – especially if they do not receive adequate help. Child abuse is not a problem that can be swept away and it craves enormous resources, both financial and emotional to tackle it seriously.

A happy childhood is every child's right. Everyone can help the next generation to be happy, safe and contented.

SOURCES OF HELP

Further information about child abuse can be obtained from:
National Society for the Prevention of Cruelty to Children (NSPCC)
67 Saffron Hill,
London EC1N 8RS.
Telephone 01-242 1626

There are local branches throughout England, Wales and Northern Ireland.

In Greater London the NSPCC runs a 24-hour child protection line for children and adults to get help with any problems, abuse or suspected abuse.
Telephone 01-404 4447

The Royal Scottish Society for the Prevention of Cruelty to Children
Melville House,
41 Polwarth Terrace,
Edinburgh EH11 1NU
Telephone 031-337 8539

ChildLine
Freepost 111
London EC4B 4BB
Freephone 0800 1111

A telephone helpline to give children counselling and help with all abuse problems.

Kidscape (KP)
82 Brook Street,
London W1Y 1YG

Free information for parents and schools on keeping safe. Programmes also available to help teach teenagers and children skills that will protect them in potentially dangerous situations.

Police and the Social Services can also be contacted in any suspected case of child abuse.

Doctors will also provide support and contacts.

WHAT THE WORDS MEAN

aggression is an attack on someone or something. It can be verbal or physical

exploitation adults using children for their own purposes and disregarding the children's interests

fractures breaks or cracks in a bone

growth retardation the slowing down of the normal growth patterns

hyperactivity unusually active behaviour, for example, being unable to sit still

incest sexual activity, including intercourse, between certain prohibited relationships, such as, father and daughter

paedophile adults who want sexual relationships with children

pornography magazines, books, photographs, videos etc, which are used to arouse adults (usually men) sexually

post mortem a medical examination carried out on a corpse to find out the cause of death

precocious behaving as if one is much older than one is

premature baby a baby born before the full term of pregnancy (nine months) has been completed

retarded child a child of low intelligence

scapegoating blaming one person or child for everything that goes wrong

self esteem the confidence one has in oneself

sexual perversion getting arousal and pleasure from things that are not usually associated with sexual pleasure

stereotype an image or pattern, where people are thought to have attitudes and beliefs in common

INDEX

Photographic Credits:
All the photographs are taken with models and obtained from the following agencies: Cover: Vanessa Bailey; pages 4, 7, 26, 32, 38, 49, 50 and 58: Rex Features; pages 9, 11, 20-21, 35, 39, 41, 47, 53 and 59: Richard and Sally Greenhill; page 12: Arkell/Network; page 14: Lewis/Network; page 18: Mary Evans; pages 23 and 25; Sturrock/Network; page 29: Hutchison Library; page 45; Abrahams/Network: page 54: Robert Harding Library.